I0628127

THE NEIGHBOR

Phoenix Poets

A SERIES EDITED BY ROBERT VON HALLBERG

MICHAEL COLLIER

the
neighbor

The University of Chicago Press
Chicago & London

The University of Chicago Press, Chicago 60637
The University of Chicago Press, Ltd., London
© 1995 by The University of Chicago
All rights reserved. Published 1995
Printed in the United States of America

04 03 02 01 00 99 98 97   2 3 4 5

ISBN 0-226-11358-2 (cloth)
ISBN 0-226-11359-0 (pbk.)

Library of Congress Cataloging–in–Publication Data

Collier, Michael, 1953–
    The neighbor / Michael Collier.
        p.   cm. — (Phoenix Poets)
    I. Title. II. Series.
    PS3553. 0474645N45 1995
    811'.54—dc20   94-21121
                                                  CIP

♾ The paper used in this publication meets the minimum requirements of the
American National Standard for Information Sciences—Permanence of Paper
for Printed Library Materials, ANSI Z39.48—1984.

for William Meredith

Why am I always the neighbor of those
who force you from fear to sing
and to say out loud: life is heavier
than the weight of all things.
Rilke, "The Neighbor"

Contents

Acknowledgments

The author is grateful to the editors of the following magazines where these poems originally appeared:

The Atlantic Monthly: "Robert Wilson" (August 1990), and "Mission Boulevard" (November 1991)

The Boston Review: "The Rancher"

The Denver Quarterly: "The House of Being" (vol. 28, no. 3 [Winter 1994], and "The Welder" (vol. 28, no. 1 [Summer 1993])

The Gettysburg Review: "Pictures Drawn by Atomic Bomb Survivors" (vol. 6, no. 4, originally "Drawings of Atomic Bomb Survivors"), reprinted by permission of the editors.

New England Review: "The Secretary," "The Raccoon," "The French Horn," and "The Water Dream" (originally "The Dream of Water")

The New Yorker: "The Barber"

Passages North: "Vietnam" and "Archimedes"

Poetry: "Breughel" (November 1992)
Raccoon: "Fröhlichkeit"
Rhetoric Review: "Baton"
Sonora Review: "Ricordo: Cittá del Vaticano" and "The Parish Fiesta"
The Southern Review: "Bread Route"

one

Archimedes

The name of the trailer
was "Lil'l Dude,"
the engine an Evinrude,
the boat a Glassport,

and under the yellow
bug-light of the carport
across the street,
my neighbor proved

his boast that with one
finger under the tongue
of the trailer,
he could lift the boat,

raise the bow as high
as his chest and haul
the rig by slow steps
onto the drive where

his pick-up idled,
and its running lights,
orange and yellow,
trimmed the camper shell.

The name of the camper
was "Six Pac," the truck
"Apache." Gerry cans
and butane tanks lashed

to the bumper and wheel
wells, and when he lowered
the trailer onto
the chrome sphere

of the hitch, the ball
and socket clicked.
He wrapped the safety
chains, like ligaments,

around the mount bolted
to the chassis, then
checked the safety
on the winch.

Inside the truck,
he eased the handbrake off
and the whole rig,
on its own, rolled

into the street.
And later, on the lake,
he held the Coleman
lantern over the dark

water, and fish rose
to it as to the sun,
a ball of gas burning
in a silk mantel, a lung

bright, reflected in the housing
glass like the source
of good to which everything
from its darkness turns—

depths of water, depths
of earth—words rising
to join their things. A flensing
knife strapped to his belt,

blade and handle shaped
like a fish and the fish
in the water,
shaped like the knife.

The Secretary

Inherited out of the house
of my father's aunt Sara,
whom he called mom,
the secretary fit
in the dark corner
of the living room,
a shrine of tiger-stripped
veneer, inlay of ivory
and mother-of-pearl.

The size of an infant's coffin,
it stood on four legs,
shoed with brass claws.
A fragile accessory
among the plaid Americana
of La-Z-Boy and sleeper couch.
Period piece, antique, relic,
and *worth-a-fortune*
were the common words

I heard describe it,
and *heirloom,* like a fabric
woven from the curious
atmosphere of its sound,
pronounced upon it
by a self-taught expert—
a cousin whose degree
had been conferred
by the School of Pretension.

In truth, the secretary
was a replica
bent on misleading us
into the drawing room
of a townhouse
we never owned.
And so it sat
for years, a tabled box
storing mother's letters,

broken decks of cards—
the family ark whose covenant,
bred of manners and mild
delusions, found its home
behind the tiny doors
and drawers that warped
and jammed. But still I found
a promise in its elegance,
a scent of pepper whenever I unfolded

the hinged top and spread
the leather blotter
tooled with silver arabesques
and stars, patterns marked out
in convoluted repetitions,
a stenciled labyrinth
from which I heard my father
calling for his mother—
a voice steady and equable

rising, unanswered, caught
in the gilded branchings
and hammered filigree
of our family.

Vietnam

The shape of it bending like an eel
or disfigured quarter moon, pink and green
and brown, like a rainbow trout. The wall

along my bed covered with the map I cut
from the newspaper, and next to it the fishing
calendar from Abonauder's Texaco. The square

cages of days with their numerals and effigies
of moon and fish shaded to indicate the shape
of the moon, the hunger of the fish.

The white bread stripped of its crust, dampened,
then dusted with flour, compressed into a tight ball,
wrapped in foil and chilled all night.

A piece of it pressed and shaped on the tip
of an Eagle Claw hook, then lowered into the nesting holes
of blue gill. The plastic bobber floating

on the surface like a silent doorbell. A whole world
of cause and effect, framed day-by-day and week-by-week.
The passage of time as a kind of game in which

I transferred numbers from the newspaper
to the calendar. The body counts and their categories
of NVRA, Marines, Montagnards.

And each morning I put a bold X through the previous
day not to erase or forget it but to connect
the corners, make four triangles of the square.

And it was rare if not impossible to catch
the blue gill that swam and swam around
the tidy pebble craters of their nests,

or coax them out except in hostile swerves
and feints toward the bait that hung
like a balloon of gravity over their homes,

a suspicious egg pouch or cocoon, something
a storm might have dislodged from the bank
and blown like a feared gift into the water,

a thing swallowed whole then run with
until the line played out and the hook set fast.

Breughel

The lump on his neck that no collar
could hide, and the charity of his presence
there in the neighborhood each fall,
door-to-door, standing in the swept porches,
waiting for the housewives to answer.

The ugly, pitiable treeman, reddish and leathery
from the sun. His baseball cap pulled tight
over his head, the visor stiff as a beaver's tail.
Year after year, the bowsaw with its wide
teeth and the long-handled loppers were all

that announced his trade. And standing on the porch
he advised nothing, though he coughed and hacked,
covering his mouth with his sap-blackened fist
and waited for the infrequent *yes* that sent him
up the trunk and into the solid lap of the branches,

where he clipped and sawed the bony leafless rigging
until the tree, all torso—lung and heart, ribs
and hips and shoulders—, stood like a knotted
goblet in the yard, a figure, as in allegory,
of his own stunted self, rooted, alive.

* * * *

My mother tried hard to convince us we were all
children of God and that the sick and maimed, the poor,
were creatures born to special destinies so unique
we could not understand. But who could understand
pain's redemptiveness and how it rarely seemed

to translate into grace. The poor were always poor,
the sick, sick—just as the treeman's goiter
did not respond to treatment, inscrutable, part
of God's plan, part of the unlovely element of love:
the humbling, the pity, the scar of violence—

a craving too frightening to name, or too tender,
the way the treeman bundled the trimmings in twine
and hauled them to the alley. And as if he counted it
his real work, leaned against the fence and with his fingers
picked the clogged sap from the blade and with a file sharpened
        the teeth.

The Temple of Light, 1972

The mower on its side in the front yard,
like a wind-up toy tipped, unable to right
itself, and the two wheels vibrating, spinning
slowly as the Briggs and Stratton chokes then dies.

And he is kneeling in his white pants, white shirt
and turbanned head, pulling out the clotted grass,
wet and thick as tea, that's jammed the blade
and made the lawn impossible to cut.

And in that telescopic, door-opening-onto-door
and window-onto-window sense, I look beyond
the Sikh, the Sufi, the gym-towel guru
into the dense physics of his hand and how

his fingers curve to fit the metal housing
and scoop the packed cuttings wedged beneath
the blade. And when it's freed he sets the mower
right and starts the engine with a single pull,

and then his hand adjusts the throttle, grips
the waist-high handle and he is lost in his purpose,
the inwarding pattern of rectangles, a doorless
labyrinth, a shutter-box effect of lawn.

And though I think I understand his purpose,
the spirit's love of discipline, the simple
obstacles of work, I see that even in his
novitiate and unlearning, he comes to anticipate

the engine's bogging down and lifts the mower
past its drowning so that the blade whirrs
at its highest speed, cutting nothing,
its motion pure, almost invisible to the eye.

And yet the eye seeing the invisible is what I remember
in his kitchen across the street as I sat
listening to him talk about the work it takes
to rise above the body's needs, about the spirit trapped

inside the mind. When he finished he offered me
a drink, and opening the refrigerator,
he reached inside for the only thing its shelves contained:
a yellow plastic pitcher that seemed to float

beneath the automatic light. Before he poured,
he turned to me and spoke as if filled
with cold illumination, "The way out is the way in."
He tipped the pitcher over paper cups, careful

to spill nothing, though there was nothing to spill,
and yet he put a cup to his lips and drank
as if his needs were never met. Months later
the logic of his conundrum came back. He'd robbed

a Circle-K—bags of Cheetos, fifty bucks.
I thought how terrified I'd been to watch him hold
the pitcher above the empty cups and how he'd fixed me
with his eye when I refused to pick mine up

and then he took it, and drank and drank.

Mission Boulevard

The headshops with their billowing cloth
canopies, red lights and bead curtains.
The girls in bikinis, trying on thin brass
bracelets, bells tied with leather straps
around their ankles. And the boys in their
baggies and jams, red and blue St. Christopher
medals around their necks. Everyone shuffling
barefoot or in water-buffalo sandals, hair
long, shaggy with salt, reddish or blond.
And there was that room in the back with black
lights where you picked out the posters
of Pig Pen and Castro, and the lady with too many
bracelets rolled them tightly into plastic sleeves.

And now years later you think what hope is there
for a secret life? or for the awkwardness
of taking out from your madras shorts the vinyl
football-shaped coin purse in which you'd carefully
folded your savings for just this purchase?
What hope is there for falling in love again
with that woman who took the money and handed back
the change smelling of incense and leather,
while you stared through the glass sales case
filled with pipes, hookahs and roach clips,
and the colorful packs of cigarette papers
displayed in a fan like the tail of an exotic bird.

The Steam Engine

Mystery of the green drapes drawn across the entrance
to the dining room. Cigarettes in brass ashtrays.
Gin in the ruby-tinted knobby crystal bottle
with its regal stopper that fit as heavy as a ball bearing

in my hand. Always in their house I felt
like a passenger who had missed his train, abandoned
in the unfamiliar scale of their living room.
The plaster roses that worked their way in chains

across the ceiling's curving vault were like incisions
on a giant's leg. Plugged with paint the petals
seemed arrested half-way in their bloom.
Whole days I spent in the great nothing-to-do

of their lives. My aunt sat with me on the floor
and traced her sun-spotted hands over the viny
and twisted patterns of her Persian rugs,
while my uncle, untethered from the green tube

of his oxygen tank, wheeled out the wobbly trolley
cart that held the steam engine: blunt black boiler
and brass connecting rods, bright steel wheels
and copper coal hopper. And in the hissing of his

tank's regulator, I heard the echo of his every breath
filling up the house, the long escaping sigh
of oxygen held off, unbreathed, so he could concentrate
on banking the tiny loaf of fuel inside the boiler grate.

And when the fuel was put in place, my aunt would light a match
beneath the grate until the pill glowed red.
Then she'd shut the boiler door and set the flue
and all of us would wait for the hiss, the steam to knot,

tightening, then knocking, so that the pistons started
shunting, sliding in their cylinders, rods and elbows
rounding on their wheels—a perfect demonstration,
a source of energy and motion that lacked a belt
or drivewheel to connect it to the world.

2212 West Flower Street

When I think of the man who lived in the house
behind ours and how he killed his wife
and then went into his own back yard,
a few short feet from my bedroom window,
and put the blue-black barrel of his 30.06
inside his mouth and pulled the trigger,
I do not think about how much of the barrel
he had to swallow before his fingers reached the trigger,
nor the bullet that passed out the back of his neck,
nor the wild orbit of blood that followed
his crazy dance before he collapsed in a clatter
over the trash cans, which woke me.

Instead I think of how quickly his neighbors restored
his humanity, remembering his passion
for stars which brought him into his yard
on clear nights, with a telescope and tripod,
or the way he stood in the alley in his rubber boots
and emptied the red slurry from his rock tumblers
before he washed the glassy chunks of agate
and petrified wood. And we remembered, too,
the goose-neck lamp on the kitchen table
that burned after dinner and how he worked
in its bright circle to fashion flies and lures.
The hook held firmly in a jeweler's vise,

while he wound the nylon thread around the haft
and feathers. And bending closer to the light,
he concentrated on tying the knots, pulling them tight
against the coiled threads. And bending closer still,
turning his head slightly toward the window,
his eyes lost in the dark yard, he took the thread ends
in his teeth and chewed them free. Perhaps he saw us
standing on the sidewalk watching him, perhaps he didn't.
He was a man so much involved with what he did,
and what he did was so much of his loneliness,
our presence didn't matter. No one's did.
So careful and precise were all his passions,

he must have felt the hook with its tiny barbs
against his lip, sharp and trigger-shaped.
It must have been a common danger for him—
the wet clear membrane of his mouth threatened
by the flies and lures, the beautiful enticements
he made with his own hands and the small loose
thread ends which clung to the roof of his mouth
and which he tried to spit out like an annoyance
that would choke him.

The House of Being

Little house it is,
little yard for exercise:
fence and alley gate,
trellis holding passion
flowers, nectar for hummingbirds
and bees, nails and crown
of thorns, ivy webbed
by trap-door spiders,
brick steps set out
at intervals, kettle
barbecue and wood pile,
deck for drinks and meals,
roses clipped, beds
pruned, driveway leading
to a closed garage;
little yard for exercise,
haftlinge clipped
and shaved; lager gate
with slogan: *Work Makes Free;*
band that welcomes back
the work details; tattooed
numbers read like names,
bunks with occupants
by twos and threes;
languages: French
and Dutch, Polish,
Yiddish—*der Dolmetscher*:
the rubber truncheon,
the interpreter.

* * * *

Little house it is
behind the house
we rent; little yard
where the woman
in her house-dress walks;
hummingbirds and spiders,
alley gate and fence,
nails and thorns,
worn path beneath
her feet, circuit
that she turns
and turns: barbecue,
garage; little yard,
little house, the past
a language she can't
misspeak: growls
and yelps, gears
of syllables and vowels,
frenzy of imperatives,
a *wortschatz* of shouts,
commands, Yiddish,
Polish, German—
der Dolmetscher
that everyone can understand.

＊＊＊＊

House of language,
little exercise
behind the house,
the woman in her dress,
her hair a whitish
gorse, she shouts
commands, frenzy
of imperatives:
Work Makes Free—
the lager gate,
trap-door spiders,
kettle barbecue,
closed garage.

two

Fröhlichkeit

After the actress
stepped from the shadows
and turned toward the camera,
you could see she was
dressed in a leather harness
and held a whip.
She picked a white rose
from a vase and slid it
behind her ear.
And then she straddled
a man who lay on the floor
sobbing. She demanded
he stop crying,
and he did, pulling himself
to a chair where he slumped
terrified, but willing
as she hooked clamps
to his nipples.
The man began crying again
and soon seemed carried
beyond tears, laughing
almost, as if to acknowledge
some sweetness in his pain,
some difficult pleasure.
Then he asked the woman,
as I think each of us

has asked a lover, *You must
hate me now?* But she,
the white rose cradled
behind her ear, rubbed
his face in the bright harness
studs circling her breasts
and said, "No, child, no.
Mother loves you. Mother
loves you." And watching
her head tilt back, mouth
open, you could hear the sounds,
as if from a human nest,
rising high and wild,
and then from his mouth, too,
as she prodded the whip
handle in his kidneys,
for joy.

The Raccoon

Outside our window we hear it licking
its paws on the fire-escape landing.
If we drew back the curtains, we'd see
its night eyes and the way it presides

over the hollow bones of a pigeon,
and how the air shaft is a vertical tunnel,
a passageway to the roof where it lives
among tar buckets and discarded mops.

Nightly we hear it praying the prayer
of paws passed over muzzle, the cleaning
and washing before it eats. We see its
shadow descending outside, beyond the opaque glass

of the bathroom window, hear the click of its nails
on the metal stairs. And what does it mean
to always see your passion embodied
in some other life, to stand near the one

who has prayed over your body and listen
together to what's beyond, what's outside,
and to know that what's missing is not something
the future will bring or time complete?

The Barber

Even in death he roams the yard in his boxer shorts,
plowing the push-mower through bermuda grass,
bullying it against the fence and tree trunks,
chipping its twisted blades on the patio's edge.

The chalky flint and orange spark of struck concrete
floats in the air, tastes like metal, smells,
like the slow burn of hair on his electric clippers.
And smelling it, I feel the hot shoe of the shaver

as he guided it in a high arc around my ears,
then set the sharp toothy edge against my sideburns
to trim them square, and how he used his huge stomach
to butt the chair and his flat hand palming my head

to keep me still, pressing my chin down as he cleaned
the ragged wisps of hair along my neck.
A fat inconsolable man whose skill and pleasure
was to clip and shear, to make raw and stubble

all that grew in this world, expose the scalp,
the place of roots and nerves and make vulnerable,
there in the double mirrors of his shop, the long
stem-muscles of our necks. And so we hung below

his license in its cheap black frame, above the violet
light of the scissors shed with its glass jars
of germicide and the long tapered combs soaking
in its blue iridescence. Gruff when he wasn't silent,

he was a neighbor to fear, yet we trusted him
beyond his anger, beyond his privacy. He was like a father
we could hate, a foil for our unspent vengeance,
though vengeance was always his. He sent us back

into the world burning and itching, alive with the horror
of closing eyes in the pinkish darkness
of his shop and having felt the horse-hair brush, talc-filled,
cloying, too sweet for boyhood, whisked across the face.

Bread Route

His name was Randy Niver and he cried so hard
the night he came to spend with me,
we had to call his mother to come and take him home,
back to the world that must have been too familiar

for him to leave: his father's boot
on the step-van grate each morning
as he climbed into the cab and closed the door
that spelled, in blue italic script, *Sunbeam*.

A blue and yellow van with a small girl's face
painted on its side, and a painted loaf of bread
sliced and the slices falling down
to make a falling, angled stack, on a blue plate.

He must have been afraid of lying where we lay,
outside, on ponchos, in sleeping bags. The sky
awash, strewn with stars, high and clear,
that let us rise above the roofs and trees.

A planet is steady light, a star blinks,
but nothing at that distance holds. Nothing
from where we lay or thought we rose
settled firm enough for sleep. And so when I no longer

could pretend not to hear him cry, I asked him
what it was. His silent answer now comes back across the years.
A friend is nothing compared with love, and love
is dark, a parent arriving in the night or leaving

each morning: a father's boot, a van door sliding shut,
bread racks empty, a clipboard waiting for its routing slips.

The Magician

Each evening he emerged from his house
with his dogs, Pepper and Cindy, leading him
slack-leashed through the neighborhood.
Pleated slacks pulled up high on his waist,

short-sleeved shirt, double pockets stuffed
with pens, and black oxfords as loose as tongues
on the sidewalk. And sometimes he wore
a hat and gray cardigan. Often we followed him

through the newly furrowed blocks of the development
down to the edge of the irrigation ditch,
where the water flowed as blue as ice all year
and the long roots of the bermuda grass trailed

in the current. When I think of him now,
I see him reaching in his pockets, the sound
of his keys and coins as he drilled a hand deeper,
searching for the magic dice, the red cup with its

disappearing ball or the pack of miniature cards.
He must have known that his hand held up to flourish
in the evening light would make whole our memory
of him, or that the Chinese handcuffs of blue

and red bamboo would amaze us, fitting loosely
on opposing fingers, a sleeve, like childhood,
hardly felt, until we tried to break away
and found our fingers locked in the weave.

He never showed us the magic of his tricks
but left us with the mystery, telling us
to pay attention to his hands which never seemed
to move, yet all the while distracted us

from their movement. And when I think
of how easily he found the nickels and quarters
behind our ears, in the cuffs of pants,
I know his magic was his silence—

words held back from explanation, gestures
deflecting us from the visible, the unseen,
as if the skill in any work is how to turn
the difficult into something plain, the plain

back into its secret, as when he said goodnight
and followed his dogs into the house.
We never saw the lights inside come on,
yet somewhere in the dark he knelt

beside the dogs, unclipped their leashes,
then standing, emptied from his pockets
the tiny vehicles of magic.

Robert Wilson

Though he is dead now and his miracle
will do us no good, I must remind myself
of what he gave, plainly,
and without guile, to all of us on the crumbling
flood-gutted bank of the Verde River
as we watched him, the fat boy,
the last one to cross, ford the violent shallows.
And how we provided him the occasion for his grace
tying his black tennis shoes to a bamboo fishing pole
and dangling them, like a simple bait,
out of reach, jerking them higher each time he rose
from his terrified crouch in the middle
of the shin-high rapids churning beneath him,
like an anger he never expressed.
And yet what moved us was not his earnestness
in trying to retrieve his shoes, nor his willingness
to be the butt of our jokes. What moved us
was how the sun struck the gold attendance star
pinned on the pocket flap of his uniform
as he fell head first
into the water and split his face,
a gash he quickly hid with his hands,
though blood leaked through his fingers as he stood
straight in the river and walked deftly toward us
out of the water to his shoes
that lay abandoned at our feet.

The Parish Fiesta

I was too young to remember this
and yet I know that I wound
through the parish fiesta above everyone,
riding on my father's shoulders,
feeling the wind eddying around my ears,
my body in tune with his steps and turns,
hands dangling at my hips or returning
the friendly waves from the food stalls
where women wrapped burritos and tacos
in red and green paper then piled them
in the steamer trays near mounds
of shredded cheese and lettuce.
I know I saw the bingo caller standing
on the varnished plywood stage
in the social hall, a lapel microphone
clipped to his white shirt, his voice
repeating the number three times,
his hand holding up the painted ping-pong
balls that popped in the glass housing
behind him. I saw the metal milk bottles
stacked in pyramids, the rows of knock-down
dolls with their battered faces,
the coin pitch for glassware and the ring toss
for transistor radios, Swiss watches,
and the illegal switch blades.
Out on the football field,

the make-shift utility poles
with their thick black wires stretched
over the village of rides—the mad mouse,
the octopus, and the carousel with its dull
blue and red neon and the garbled music
that rose and fell with each horse's smooth glide.
And in the passageway between the school buildings,
I watched the young pastor ease his white
pasty body onto the metal saddle
above the choppy water of the dunking booth,
his face protected by a wire grille,
his hands rigid at his sides, unable to grip
the seat that would dump him again and again
into the shallow trough of water below.
And I remember holding the soggy softball,
almost too heavy, handing it to my father below,
who tilted as he side-armed it
into the target to drop the priest.
And finally, as if this were the reason
for memory's long list of particulars,
for its fair lies, its true distortions,
I remember the man who took the pastor's place,
how he stood shivering in his dry bathing suit,
and the cigarette he sent hissing into a puddle,
then the seed of spit from his mouth,
the little pearl that answered his obligation,
floating thick and white in the day's overspill.

for William Maxwell

Whistler

Not a tune, not melody or notes
but something like death's rattle,
constantly we heard it, day and night,
as he shuffled through the camp site.
A bailiff for the county court,
he walked like a jailer from tent

to tent, pausing, not to hear
the subversive sleeplessness within
but to feel our presence and count
by twos our feigning heads.
We feared him not the way we feared
our parents, but the way we feared

authority and how it found itself
embodied in his deformity:
the S of his spine, head cocked
like an attentive bird's, the twisted
rail yard of suture marks down his back.
And in the morning when he shaved,

shirtless, over the barrel of wood-
fired water, he held the metal
shaving mirror in one hand, razor
in the other, and dragged the hard
sides of his face, and all the while
he struggled, whistling, sounding

like a whisper, a tune, a rasp,
a contentment, a preoccupation
always escaping, or a nonchalance
eyeing our conspiracies that gathered,
under his long nose which he said
could smell our shit before we made it.

The Rancher

When he rises from his naugahyde recliner
to shake your hand, he cups his fingers
behind his ear to catch your name.
He grips your hand to see if you're man

enough to date his daughter, and though
you're barely man enough, you've got
the strength to pass his test.
You meet his eyes that know exactly

how to judge a lamb or yearling's face
and what he sees in yours he doesn't trust.
How could he? When his daughter's dressed
and wearing make-up, he calls her cheap,

a floozie. His wife's her pimp.
He's not *bad,* his daughter tells you.
*We're all women in this house, that's hard
on him, and Mom's such a bitch.*

When he's drunk, he comes into her room
with what she calls his badger's muzzle
and sniffs her neck and shoulders.
But what's worse, she tells you, is when

she comes home from her dates and if he's
still awake, he lifts her dress or puts
his hand inside her Levis. And so each time
you came to pick her up, he looked at you

as both the one who'd save his daughter
and use her. He told you once, *she lies*
don't trust her, and then, as if to prove it,
he led you to the service porch,

where a freezer, as large as a grave casing,
paralleled his beat-up truck. He propped
the freezer open with a piece of 2x4,
high enough so that the light inside

illumined rows and stacks of plastic bags,
clear, the contents burred with ice.
Each one contained what looked to you
like scallops, though larger. He reached inside

and knocked a bag loose with his fist,
then picked it up and said, *She'll do to you*
what I did to sheep to get these,
then threw the bag back in, closed the lid,

slapped you on the ass and squeezed you,
hard. You felt the badger's muzzle then,
prickly and wiry, his cheek like a shaved pelt,
and then heard what he said, a whisper,

You tell me what it's like with her
and I'll be glad to listen.

three

The Fairy Tale

When the jewels spilled to the floor
of their father's house, the story ended:
perversion and treachery endured, rewarded.
The best way to send children to bed—
fright overcome, but lingering. And a duck
paddling across the pond to save them.

But what if the story didn't end there?
The stepmother not dead, a divorcee
whose alimony was half her husband's
weekly crust of bread, and the witch hadn't burned?
What if like everywhere else in the world
of dread, the past grew larger each day?

Then despite his children's return,
the father never forgives himself.
The stepmother arrives with her lawyer
to put a lien on the jewels. While
the witch, disguised as a kind old lady,
files a countersuit, and the duck swims

in the park pond and waits for the children's
song. But the shore is dark and the children
are out collecting pebbles, for they hear
the adults plotting in sadness and greed
once more to obscure the way from the woods
to the house. But the lien against the heart's

true strength holds the guile that waits,
as the child waits, for the chance to push
the witch into the oven and escape
with her brother to her father's house
where the fright overcome overcomes them again.

Baton

I switch spindles—45 to 33—
and change the platter speed,
then reverse the needle's plastic lever
to read LP, and there in the alcove
of the living room, I work by feel
to match the album's tiny hole
with the spindle's rounded top,
then swing the stiff forearm
of the record guide to hold the disc
in place. Absorbed in mastering
the machine, I don't hear my grandmother
shuffling her stroke-stuttered feet
as she leaves the back bedroom.
The album drops in a whoosh,
the platter turns and whines,
the tone arm rises jerkily
then drops its single diamond tooth
into the microscopic grooves
that echo again and again
the Major Motion Picture Soundtrack:
The High and the Mighty.
And still unknown to me, Grandmother
leans against the bookshelf planter
that divides living room from hall
and watches as I lift my arms,
my fingers pinching the ends

of imaginary batons,
my shoulders toed-in, cocked to fire
against the first percussive chords
and imitate the broad dramatic gestures
of the orchestra's conductor—the man
who on the album cover slashes
and carves the air and puts
a kind of fear into the mantis-like
musicians stationed in their chairs.
And when the music fills the hi-fi's
massive woofer, I stand on toes
and lean into the volume as if it were
a blast of air that lifts me off the ground.
But then deep inside the music
like a desperate signal escaping
from the pin-prick of lights glowing
from the amplifier's rows of vacuum tubes,
I hear Grandmother's cough, and turning
find her bent, half-standing in the hall,
her hands held up in counterpoint to mine,
her hair an unreal shade of blue,
and as I drop my hands, she shakes
her ghastly head—a motion that cuts
through all pretense.

Ricordo: Città del Vaticano

Gravity governs the changing of these guards
who slide through the plastic barrel
of a souvenir pen, an ounce of mineral oil
the timely element that lets them cross,

from portico to portico, the entrance
of St. Peter's Square. And having crossed,
I send them back again—heads in front
of halberds—by tilting down the pen.

And so, trapped in their slow though never-
changing world, and dressed in couture
by Raphael or Michelangelo, they govern
all the words that live unwritten

inside the plastic vein of ink.
The names and streets, the world's
four lines that make addresses
complete or incomplete and make

the off-hand greetings (*wish you could
be here, miss you, I'll write when
I've more time, the light this evening
was . . .*) more like the thoughts that guard

our thoughts and keep us safe or far
enough removed from the true sentiment
we feel when, lira in hand, we lean across
the simonist's stall to buy a gift,

a tiny machine for writing, almost holy,
almost blest, a sure emblem of the heart's kitsch.

Drill

When the fire bell rang its two short, one long
electric signal, the boys closest to the wall
of windows had to raise the blinds and close
the sashes, and then join the last of our line
as it snaked out the classroom onto the field
of asphalt where we stood, grade-by-grade,
until the principal appeared with her gold Timex.

We learned early that catastrophe must always
be attended in silence, that death prefers us
orderly and ordered, and that rules will save us
from the chaos of our fear, so that even
if we die, we die together, which was the calm
almost consoling thought I had each time
the yellow C.D. siren wailed and we would tuck
ourselves beneath our sturdy desktops.

Eyes averted from the windows,
we'd wait for the drill to pass or until
the nun's rosary no longer clicked and we could hear
her struggling to free herself from the leg-well
of her desk, and then her call for us to rise
and, like herself, brush off the dust gathered
on our clothes. And then the lessons resumed.
No thought of how easily we interred ourselves,

though at home each would dream the mushroom cloud,
the white cap of apocalypse whose funnel stem
sucked glass from windows, air from lungs,
and made all these rehearsals the sad and hollow
gestures that they were, for we knew it in our bones
that we would die, curled in a last defense—
head on knees, arms locked around legs—
the way I've seen it since in nursing homes

and hospices: forms bedsheets can't hide,
as if in death the body takes on the soul's
compact shape, acrobatic, posed to tumble free
of the desktop or bed and join the expanse
and wide scatter of debris.

The Welder

This evening driving over the narrow metal bridge
of the Broadkill River and listening to the mallards
honking from the bamboo and pussywillow of the marsh—
the herons staked to the island mudflats , I almost missed
the match-flare sun in the rear-view mirror, going
down behind me, darkening the cornfields and lighting
for the last of that long day the pine windbreak.

And in the orange burst and flare, I saw the dark
splayed figure of my high-school friend dropping down
out of the white sky, a black heavy cross falling toward
the rising and flattening earth where his father,
standing in the landing field among the bright cloth X's
of targets, followed the descent through binoculars.
His son so intent on the ripcord and safety chute

showed no panic in his face, no fear, though he never opened it
before he disappeared behind the line of trees bordering the road.
And imagining his father standing in the field, his hand
held up against the shocking white of the sky, I think
of when I stood on the brick patio behind their house
and watched his father fit the cylindrical welder's helmet
over his fat bald head, the visor raised while he clamped

the ground strap to the fence and fit his hands
with blackened, rough-out gloves. And though
we handed him the welding rods and scrubbed slag
from the fresh seams, with a wirebrush, we could not look
directly at the flame's blue snap, the white electric drizzle
but found it muted in the corner of the visor,
a blue and white reflection dulled to yellow in the black glass,

a star burning and glowing in its moment of creation
before it disappeared on the horizon—a slow
hiss of escaping gas, light fast and precise
that dwarfed us as it passed.

Pictures Drawn by Atomic Bomb Survivors

Catalogs of the burned: people, telephone poles,
steam engines, wires, pigs, horses—many horses.
And the smashed: windows, buildings, wagons, cars,
streetcars. And the screaming: children for mothers,
mothers for children, pleas for help, water, food.

All of this set down by amateurs thirty years later,
makes the "compelling subject" more symbolic
than real, a legend that never lives up to its facts:
how the day went dark, a black rain fell, and the air
sucked out from the air left a hollow silence before

the wind returned, a Typhoon of black, burned
and splintered things, flames from the nonflammable.
As well as strange apocalyptics: a cow's tail hanging on a wire.
A man, naked, standing in the dark rain, holding an eye
in one of his hands. All of it no stranger than a dream,

except it was no dream's strangeness to wake from,
no place in the world's future from which we might look
and see a hand, fingertips on fire, blue flames,
the fingers like candles burning to their joints,
a dark liquid running to the ground along the wrist.

Or how the larger destruction concealed the smallest regret:
a girl's scissors and lunchbox scattered
on her class-room floor, and the girl, after the blast,
picking herself up, sees them. And now beneath her
drawing writes: "Why didn't I stretch my hands out

to take them? Those scissors sent by a friend in Hawaii.
They were sharp, shiny, and would never rust."

Letter from Mrs. C. G. Vogt

I saw Crane, swimming strongly. . . . It is a
scene I am unable to forget, even after all
these years, and now I am glad to know why that
tortured man made such a decision.

These great and gentle violent flaws,
like waves that build to peaks and break,
are not the explanation for our acts
but rather the source of those
compelling tortured things that reside in us
from birth. And so, if at the time

I saw him emerge on the Orizaba's deck—
topcoat over his pajamas—and watched him fold
his coat over the ship's rail and place
both hands along it and then raise himself
on his toes, and then drop back again,
before he vaulted over the railing

into the sea, if at that time I had known
the two "earliest surviving photographs
of Harold Hart Crane," I might have seen
in one his final frontward pose already
practiced—the child at twelve months
acquiring his balance from the arm of a chair.

And in the other, set already on the obscure mystery
of leaving, his back turned, head cocked down,
as he leans over a stool as if to watch
the buoys and lifeboats lowered to his grown
and desperate self, which he saw, swimming strongly,
and as if forever though never again.

The French Horn

Almost mute in the night shadows
of his gabled room, we lay awake
in adjoining beds while the shape
of the instrument he'd shown me
before the lights went out
floated in the air, free
of the vacant inverse of its case.

It hovered above me like a brass Q,
a letter whose magnitude was not
of brightness but of dimension:
clefts and serifs, finger holes
and stops, the velvet washers
covering the valves. An elegance
that took the spit and sputter

of my cousin's lips, a tune
like a story struggling to cohere,
arranging scales and patterns,
a way of bringing sleep near.
But when I woke, lost in the unaccustomed
night and heard my cousin dreaming,
his voice a cramp of terror,

the room a coffin's shape of dark,
except the clock face floating
on his bureau, all at once I knew
where I was sleeping: his younger
brother's bed, a cousin I had never met—
mongoloid or retarded, a condition
I could only suspect. We were a family

practiced in its hidings: my mother's
mother institutionalized for fifty years.
The math is overwhelming: she died
at ninety. And yet those
who would want her back can't have her,
who would want the years when she
was only frail and feeble can't have them either.

It's been thirty years since I looked
inside my cousin's music case.
The horn lay as still as God's heart,
and my cousin let me hold the mouthpiece
in my hand: a metal eye and optic stem.
Nothing so small has ever felt that cold
or on a humid night been so difficult to warm.

The Water Dream

Courage from my oldest son
who wore the tanks and mask
whose feet were purple webs,

whose eyes, blue behind the oval
lens, shone bold. His hair
a yellow sponge wrapped around

the regulator gauge. Outside
the world of dream he would have drowned,
and so I wondered at the graceful

flutter of his kick and how he bore
the apparatus, wore the leaded belt
and where he learned his skill,

or how he knew to circle there
where sand shelved off to rocks,
and where the rocks shimmered

in bottom light—an orange murk
of shape and bulk to which he pointed
with a gig, short-handled, meant

for frogs. And then he surfaced,
and turning on his back so he could lift
the mask, he said, *Mother is near.*

Then he dove and disappeared,
and in his absence something cold rose:
the feeling of an empty place

where fear intrudes, where death becomes
the dreamer's death or where an animal
long-tame, transforms into a beast.

But where I swam, I heard the turbines
of the dam whine and hum along the bottom
of the lake—a sound, like pressure

in the ears, a sound of crushing weight,
a thing almost too literal to dream,
an exit song where light answered light,

and where I rose to the conscious shore,
feet down, dry above the edge of the reservoir,
and where I heard a voice inside me say,

Go out, go out and walk on the water
as if on the meniscus of this dream. Shadow
the shadow movement of your son.

But in the dream I never rose,
and all at once I found myself
beneath black water, made blacker

by the hull that bobbed above me.
The boat that held my family—
father, mother, sisters—stuck

at anchor, and the anchor lodged
in dark. What son would not
acquiesce to the danger and carry

with him the anger that neutralized
his fear, pocket his blame,
like air, against his father

for having been sent down to do a job
his father should have done
and finding it impossible to do,

come up a gasping failure?
And what little company
I would have needed to give me

courage. What shadow presence
came last and late and with impatience:
a knife handed down to me, a sharp

blade and raw-hide handle to cut
the line and watch the boat turn
its stern to me, while the brass prop

unwound slowly in the drift,
and the hand above reached down
to take the knife.